Victory With Vica LLC

Legal & Credit Repair Services

www.victorywithvica.com

Preparing for the Real World
Workbook (Grades 1-4)

Written by Lavica M. Chandler

Illustrated by Antonio Collins

Transformed

Romans 12:2 Publishing

www.transformedpublishing.com

transformed Publishing

Mission: To Proclaim Transformation and Truth

Published by: Transformed Publishing

Website: www.transformedpublishing.com

Email: transformedpublishing@gmail.com

Illustrated by Antonio Collins—Cocoa, FL
Timeless Photography Plus

Cover Photography by Saraellen Bagby—Richmond, VA
JBella Photography: jbellaphotography.zenfolio.com

ISBN: 978-1-953241-09-2
Printed in the U.S.A.

Dedication

This workbook is dedicated to Israel, Reign, Joshua, and Jasauni.

Table of Contents

Table of Contents

Introduction

Victory with Vica LLC Educational Resources, Volume I

Preparing for the Real World Workbook (Grades 1-4)

This workbook is designed to teach children how to create a lifetime plan towards learning specific methods about spending and saving, budgeting, separating their wants and needs, and how to overcome overspending.

Included in this workbook:

$ **Real World Scenarios**

$ **Activity Worksheets**

$ **Reward Sheet**

$ **Certificate of Excellence**

$ Stickers are included with direct purchases from victorywithvica.com

$ For third party purchases, please provide stickers for each child

The Savings Jar

Key Word Definitions:

$ **Income -** The amount of money earned from working hard

$ **Save -** To put aside income or funds from working hard

$ 60

Israel and Joshua are looking at their iPad for a new basketball goal that costs no more than $60.00.

How much money do Israel and Joshua have in their savings jars? Israel thinks they have saved enough money to buy a new basketball goal and Joshua thinks they have not saved enough money. Let's find out who is correct.

The Savings Jar Activity

Help Israel and Joshua find the total amount of money they have if they combine their savings jars.

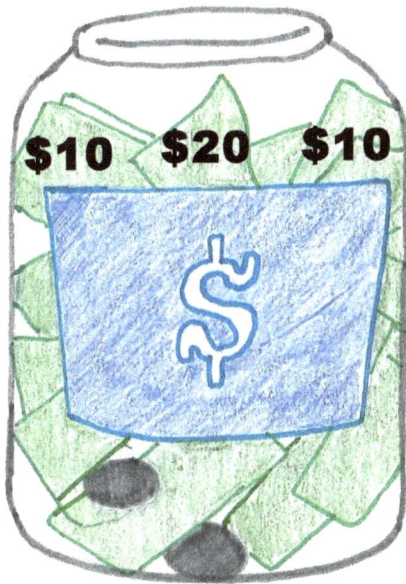

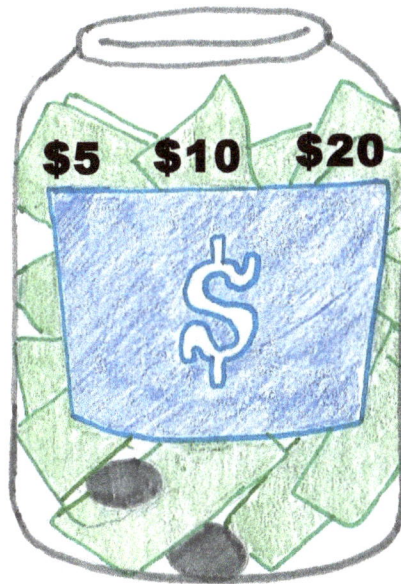

$10 $20 $10

$5 $10 $20

Activity Questions:

1. At this time, how much money have Israel and Joshua saved altogether?

   _____

2. Are they able to purchase the basketball goal?

   _____

3. Who was correct, Israel or Joshua?

   _____

Great job champ! Enjoy a reward sticker of your choice!

My Savings Planning Sheet

Directions:

$ Create your savings plan!

$ Please ask for help from your parent or guardian.

1. I am saving for _____.

2. My savings goal is $_____.

3. How much will I save weekly? $_____

4. How long will it take me to reach my personal savings goal?

_____

5. The 3 ways I will earn money to reach my personal goal are:

_____

_____

_____

6. Did I reach my personal goal? _____

It's okay superstar if you have to adjust your goals.
You are limitless!

4

The Budget Builder

Key Word Definitions:

$ **Budget -** A strategic plan for saving and spending money wisely

$ **Cost -** The price paid for an individual item

$ **Decision -** Making a choice after thinking it through

$150

Reign wants a brand new rose gold scooter that costs $150. She asked her parents if they would purchase the scooter for her. Instead, her parents offered her a summer job to work and earn her own money.

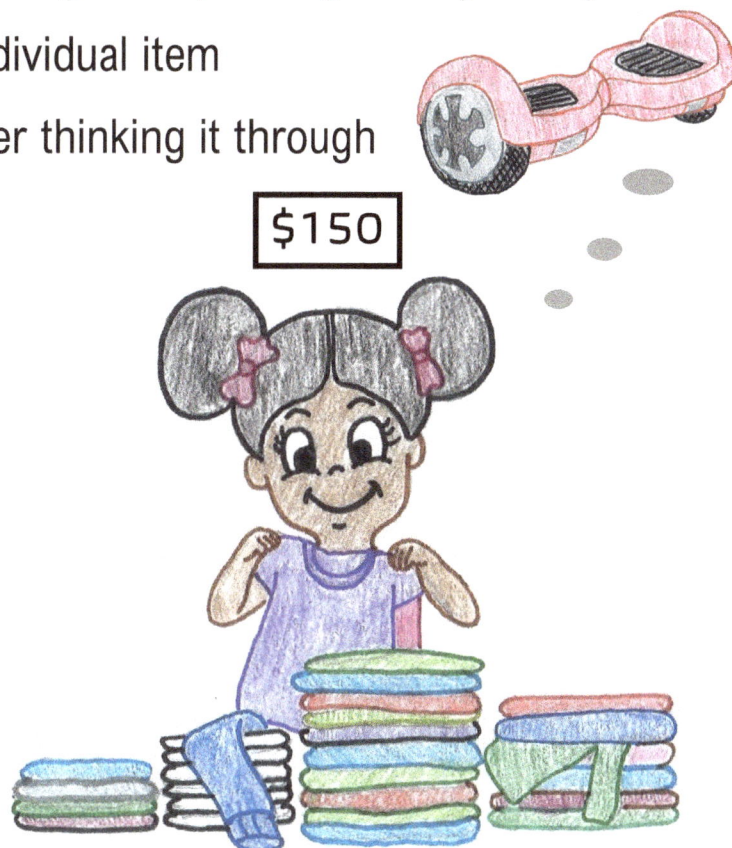

During Reign's first week of working, her chores consisted of organizing laundry and decluttering.

Activity Question:

Reign practiced budgeting. She earned $50 per week. Of that $50, she decided to save $30 per week to meet her savings goal of $150.

How many weeks will it take for Reign to save enough money to buy the brand new rose gold scooter she wants? _____

Outstanding brainstorming skills budget master! You Rock! Ask your parent/guardian if you can help them with the laundry next time.

What Did I Just Learn?

$ Being a dedicated worker allows me to earn income.

$ Building a budget, saving, and spending my money wisely teaches me how to responsibly purchase the things I need now and the things I may want later.

$ I will remember to have fun and spend my money responsibly.

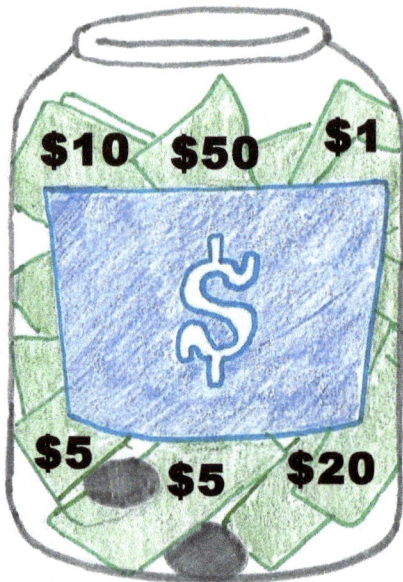

Word Search

Directions:

Circle or highlight each word from the Word Box in the Word Search below:

$ Word Box $

save	cost	goal
income	money	work
decision	budget	earn
spend	manage	afford
job	purchase	

A	F	F	O	R	D	C	X	P
A	S	A	V	E	B	O	E	U
Z	A	C	W	B	V	S	A	R
L	I	J	O	B	C	T	R	C
D	E	C	I	S	I	O	N	H
P	P	H	R	Y	N	G	S	A
B	U	D	G	E	T	O	T	S
I	D	M	K	N	J	A	O	E
Y	F	M	R	O	I	L	L	E
I	N	C	O	M	E	F	J	S
Q	B	Q	W	S	P	E	N	D
W	G	M	A	N	A	G	E	C

What I Want vs. What I Need

Key Word Definitions:

$ **Wants** - Things you can live without, but are nice to have

$ **Needs** - Things that are required for survival

| $60 | $75 | $100 | $95 |

Moe saw a skateboard in the mall he wants that cost $100. He went into another store and saw a pair of shoes that he needed for $25, but there was a really cool pair of shoes that he wanted in the same store that cost $75. The last store he went into had a $30 jacket he needed for the winter, but there was a really nice jacket that had his favorite character on it that cost $85! He also needed a new pair of jeans. He found a pair of jeans on sale for $24, but a name brand pair that he wanted for $64 were displayed in the store window. Moe has some decisions to make about how he will spend his money. Help Moe determine which items are wants and which items are needs.

Activity:

List the 4 items that Moe WANTS:

1.
2.
3.
4.

List the 3 items Moe NEEDS:

1.
2.
3.

What is the TOTAL COST if Moe purchases all the things he wants:

_____

What is the TOTAL COST if Moe ONLY purchases the things he needs:

_____

Excellent Job take 2 reward stickers and pat yourself on the back!

8

Let's Work Together

Directions:

$ With your parent / guardian, create a list of things that you want and a list of things you need.

$ Next time you are at the store, help find the items needed on the list.

Activity:

What I want:

_____
_____
_____
_____
_____
_____
_____
_____
_____
_____
_____
_____
_____
_____
_____
_____
_____

What I need:

_____
_____
_____
_____
_____
_____
_____
_____
_____
_____
_____
_____
_____
_____
_____
_____
_____

Pick out your favorite reward sticker! You deserve it!

Overcome Overspending

Key Word Definitions:

$ **Overcome** – To gain control

$ **Overspend -** To spend beyond one's budget

Directions:

Bryson has to overcome overspending. He has a budget of $80. Help Bryson by circling items he can afford without going over the budget that his parents gave him.

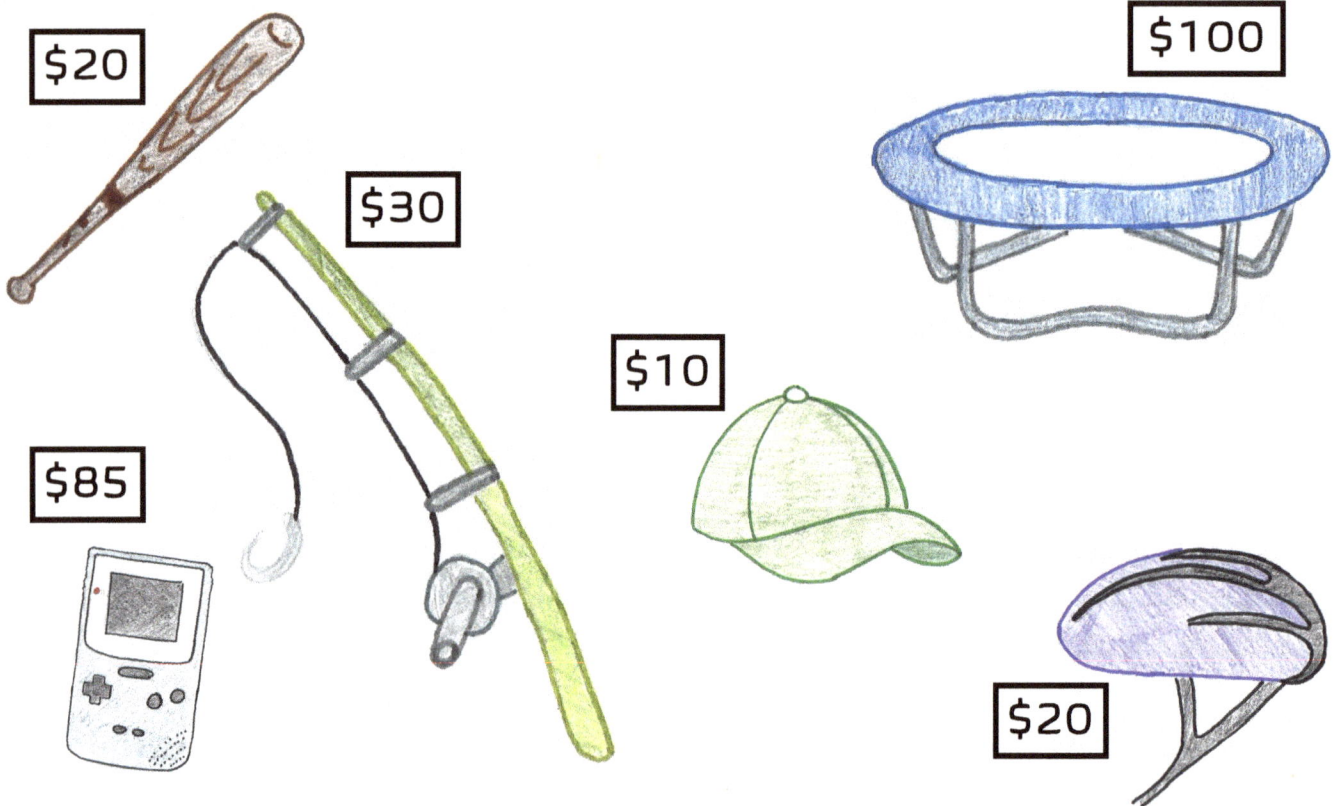

$20

$30

$100

$10

$85

$20

Activity Question:

What items can Bryson purchase without overspending?

_____

Grab yourself a reward sticker, you are doing great!

Money Maze

Directions:

$ Let's have more fun! Jump into the money maze and see how much money you can find.

$ Write each amount you find as you go.

START

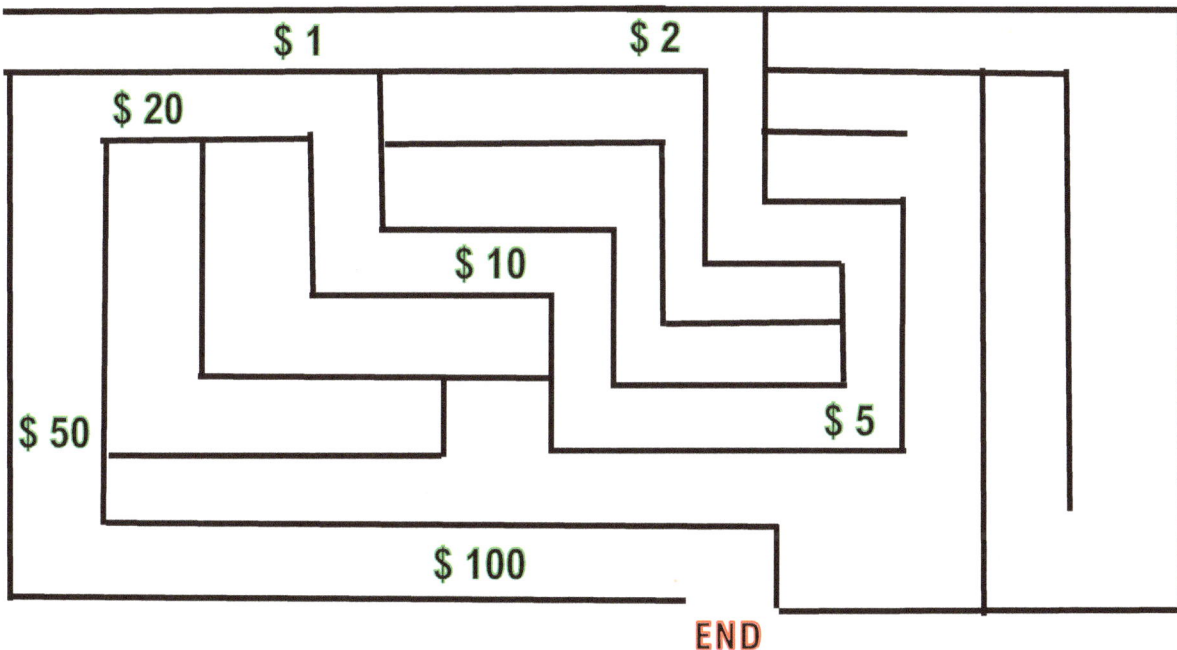

$ 1 $ 2

$ 20

$ 10

$ 50

$ 5

$ 100

END

Amount #1:_____

Amount #2:_____

Amount #3:_____

Amount #4:_____

Amount #5:_____

Amount #6:_____

Amount #7:_____

Total Amount:_____

You are amazing!

How to Prepare for the Real World

$ Hopefully, you have enjoyed the activities throughout this workbook.

$ Here is a quick overview of what you've learned:

$ Saving reduces your need to borrow money.

$ You must plan how you will distribute your money.

$ Building a budget teaches you how to responsibly purchase your wants and needs.

$ You overcome overspending by simply learning from prior mistakes and creating better spending habits.

Words You Have Learned

Glossary:

Key Word: Definition:

$	**Afford**	Having enough money to pay for an item
$	**Budget**	A strategic plan for saving and spending money wisely
$	**Cost**	The price paid for an individual item
$	**Decision**	Making a choice after thinking it through
$	**Income**	The amount of money earned from working hard
$	**Needs**	Things that are required for survival
$	**Overcome**	To gain control
$	**Overspend**	To spend beyond one's budget
$	**Save**	To put aside income or funds from working hard
$	**Wants**	Things you can live without, but are nice to have

You have learned so much!
You are preparing yourself for financial success in the real world!

Activity Answer Sheet

Lesson:

The Savings Jar, pg. 3

The Budget Builder, pg. 5

Word Search, pg. 7

Answers:

1. $75   2. yes   3. Israel

5 weeks

```
A F F O R D C     P
  S A V E     O E U
          S A R
      J O B   T R C
  D E C I S I O N H
        Y   G   A
  B U D G E T O S
    K N     A   E
    R O     L
· I N C O M E
    W S P E N D
  M A N A G E
```

What I Want vs. What I Need, pg. 8

<u>Wants:</u> $100 skateboard, $75 shoes, $85 jacket, & $64 jeans = $324.

<u>Needs:</u> $25 shoes, $30 jacket, & $24 jeans = $79

Overcoming Overspending, pg. 10

Have a parent help you add up your purchases.
Is the total less than $80?
If so, you stayed within your budget.

Money Maze, pg. 11

$1, $2, $5, $10, $20, $50, $100 = $188

You have learned so much!

14

About the Author

Thank you for taking the time to complete the *Preparing for the Real World Workbook!*

Victory with Vica LLC was established in January 2017 during a time when I was facing my own credit adversities. I was expecting my first child. I knew, for my personal situation, a newer vehicle was needed, a bigger home was required, and a better future had to be designed for my expanding family.

Through research, planning, and action I was able transform my credit and build the financial stability necessary for my family. My desire is to pass this essential financial literacy on to others.

The Office of Victory with Vica LLC specializes in educating consumers about unverifiable and misleading debt, such as, medical bills, credit card debt, collections, bankruptcy, charge offs, student loans, wage garnishment cancellations, debt settlements and negotiations, and much more! We acknowledge the unique situation of each client and their personal credit goals.

Please visit our website to schedule a consultation. We are located in VA, but work virtually with clients throughout the U.S.A.

Business Location:
316 Main Street
South Boston, VA 24592

Business Phone Number:
(434) 404-3427

Business Website:
victorywithvica.com

Victory With Vica LLC
Legal & Credit Repair Services

Reward Sheet

Directions:

$ Place YOUR Reward Stickers on this page each time you earn one!

$ You are accomplishing so much. Thank you for your hard work!

Certificate *of* Excellence

Presented to

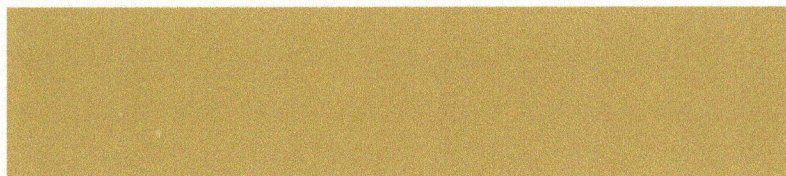

for

Successful Completion of
Preparing for the Real World

Congratulations!
I am Proud of You!
- Lavica M. Chandler

www.ingramcontent.com/pod-product-compliance
Lightning Source LLC
Chambersburg PA
CBHW052347210326
41597CB00037B/6285